D0927027

For Mother, who always thought I could
—A.I.
For my two sweet-toothed kids
—M.B.

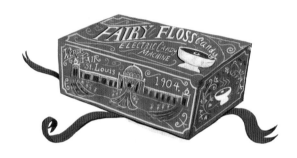

 little bee books

An imprint of Bonnier Publishing USA
251 Park Avenue South, New York, NY 10010
Text copyright © 2017 by Ann Ingalls
Illustrations copyright © 2017 by Migy Blanco
All rights reserved, including the right of reproduction in whole or in part in any form.
LITTLE BEE BOOKS is a trademark of Bonnier Publishing USA, and associated
colophon is a trademark of Bonnier Publishing USA.
Manufactured in China   LEO 1116
First Edition 10 9 8 7 6 5 4 3 2 1
ISBN 978-1-4998-0238-2
Library of Congress Cataloging-in-Publication Data
Names: Ingalls, Ann, author. | Blanco, Migy, illustrator.
Title: Fairy Floss / by Ann Ingalls; illustrated by Migy Blanco.
Description: New York: Little Bee Books, [2017] | First Edition.
Identifiers: LCCN 2016014966 | Subjects: | CYAC: Louisiana Purchase Exposition
(1904: Saint Louis, Mo.)—Fiction. | Inventors—Fiction.
Saint Louis (Mo.)—History—20th century—Fiction.
Classification: LCC PZ7.I45 Fai 2017 | DDC [E]—dc23
LC record available at https://lccn.loc.gov/2016014966

littlebeebooks.com
bonnierpublishingusa.com

JUN 09 2017

FAIRY FLOSS

THE SWEET STORY of Cotton Candy

DALTON FREE PUBLIC LIBRARY
DALTON, MASSACHUSETTS 01226

by
Ann Ingalls

illustrated by
Migy Blanco

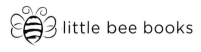 little bee books

Lillie and her aunt Mae watched as John Wharton, the candymaker, stood over a gas-fired stove. He turned the crank on his candy-making machine over and over again.

"Making spun sugar sure is hard work," said Lillie. "When will it be done?"

"It's almost ready," replied John. "As the little barrel spins faster and faster, melted sugar passes through tiny openings and into the catching bowl. It cools and forms candy thread."

"Look! It's starting to do that now," said Lillie.

A few minutes later, Lillie and Aunt Mae tasted the spun sugar.

"Mmm," said Lillie.

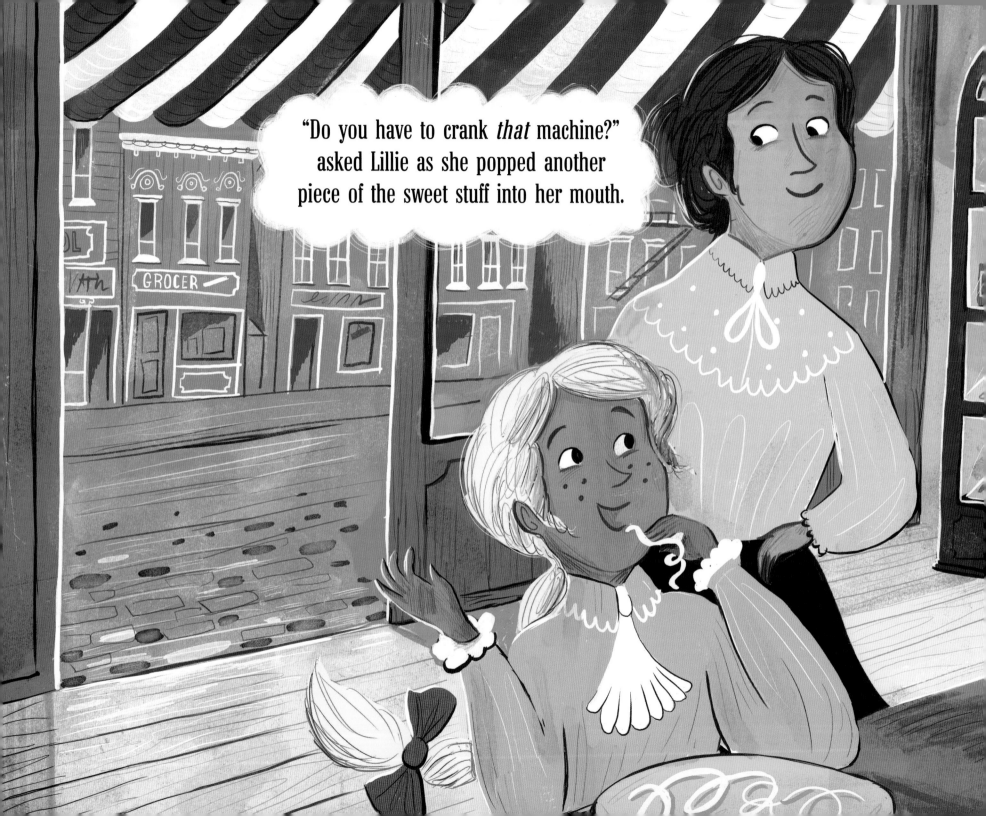

"No, we don't," said John. "William added an electric motor that does it for us. People all over the world have been making spun sugar as thick as string for hundreds of years. But the candy our new machine makes is as fine as thread. We call it fairy floss."

"I can't wait to see it!" said Lillie.

A few days later, small sparks flew off the tracks as Lillie and Aunt Mae hopped off the electric cable car. They had arrived at the 1904 St. Louis World's Fair! What a lollapalooza!

"There are so many things to see!" said Lillie.
"Mr. Ferris's wheel, motorcars, moving pictures...
Why, there is even an indoor skating rink—in the summer!
But most of all, I want to see John Wharton and
William Morrison and their electric candy machine."

"Look at all the electric lights, Lillie," said Aunt Mae.
"As far as the eye can see! How will we ever find
the electric candy machine?"

"Mr. Wharton said to look for them at the Palace of Electricity,"
said Lillie, peering through the crowd of people.
"Look—there it is!"

As they walked over, Lillie and Aunt Mae strolled past Cascade Gardens.

"That looks like so much fun! Can we do that?" Lillie asked.

"Why not?" Aunt Mae said with a smile.
"Let's come back after we see the electric candy-making machine."

When they reached the Palace of Electricity, they saw electric typewriters, coffeemakers, toasters, bread machines, and dishwashers.

They had never seen so many gadgets!

Crowds of people filled the room. It was impossible to see very far. Then Lillie smelled something toasty and sweet, like caramels. It made her mouth water.

And there were John and William at their stand, derby hats perched on their heads. They wore starched collars, bow ties, and aprons.

William winked at Lillie, but he couldn't stop to talk. He was too busy. He spun batch after batch of fairy floss. It was white and fluffy and seemed to float in the bowl.

"It looks like food for fairies," Lillie said.

When the crowd finally cleared, John called to Lillie. "Would you like to make some fairy floss?"

"Yes, sir!" said Lillie, hopping onto a stool.

William handed Lillie a small cup of sugar. "This is the magic ingredient."

With William's help, Lillie poured the sugar into the little barrel inside the shiny floss bowl.

Then John said, "When I press this button, the machine will start."

Just as soon as he did, the machine made a rumbling sound. The barrel began to turn around and around, and the sugar began to melt.

Soon glassy threads of sugar piled up in the bowl. Before long, fluffy clouds of candy began to spin out of the barrel.

It looked like the fairy floss would flow over the sides and onto the floor! But John didn't let that happen.

He quickly twirled the floss on a long-handled fork. Then he tucked it into a wooden box and handed it to Lillie.

"Here's your first batch, young lady," said William.

Lillie pulled some coins from her pocket, but William stopped her.

Lillie opened up the box,
pinched off a bit of the candy,
and tossed it in her mouth.

"Mmm . . . it's so good
and magical—like fairy dust!"

"And what do you think of our invention?" asked William.

"Your machine is a real razzle-dazzle," replied Lillie. "It's the sweetest thing at the fair."

Author's Note

The Electric Candy Machine was invented in 1897 by William Morrison, a dentist, and John C. Wharton, a candymaker. It melted sugar and spun it through tiny holes in a barrel that rotated quickly. The sugar cooled into sweet threads of candy and was collected in a large bowl.

Before this invention, making fairy floss was hot, hard work. Most machines were operated with a hand crank or a foot pedal, and the sugar was melted over a gas fire.

In 1899, William Morrison and John Wharton obtained a patent for their machine. One year later, these machines were sold to candy stores.

Their machine for creating "fairy floss" was introduced in 1904 at the St. Louis World's Fair. It sold for 25 cents a box. They sold 68,655 boxes.

Cotton candy is popular all over the world. It has been given a variety of names. In Poland, it is called sugar cotton (*wata cukrowa*); in Germany, sugar wool (*Zuckerwatte*); and in France, father's beard or papa's beard (*barbe à papa*). In other places it is known as breeze cotton, pinkie floss, candy feathers, candy cloud, spun sugar, candy floss, and candy fluff.

National Cotton Candy Day is December 7.

For Further Reading

"1904 World's Fair Collection." *Missouri History Museum*.
 http://www.mohistory.org/lrc/collections/objects/1904-worlds-fair-collection.

"Cotton Candy: The Toothy History of a Classic Circus Treat." *Historic Hudson Valley*. May 24, 2012.
 http://www.hudsonvalley.org/community/blogs/cotton-candy-toothy-history-classic-circus-treat.

Christen, A. G., and J. A. Christen. "William J. Morrison (1860-1926): Co-Inventor of the Cotton Candy Machine."
 http://www.ncbi.nlm.nih.gov/pubmed/16092607.
 Patent information.

Crockett, Zachary. "How a Dentist Popularized Cotton Candy." *Priceonomics*. September 3, 2014.
 http://priceonomics.com/how-a-dentist-popularized-cotton-candy/.

Gaskins III, Lee E. "Food Facts and Fallacies." *At the Fair: The Grandness of the 1904 World's Fair*.
 http://atthefair.homestead.com/Misc/FoodFactFalalcies.html.

Wilpert, Chris Von. "History of Fairy Floss: How They Spun It Back in the 'Floss Age.'" *Snowy Joey*.
 http://snowyjoey.com.au/history-of-fairy-floss/.

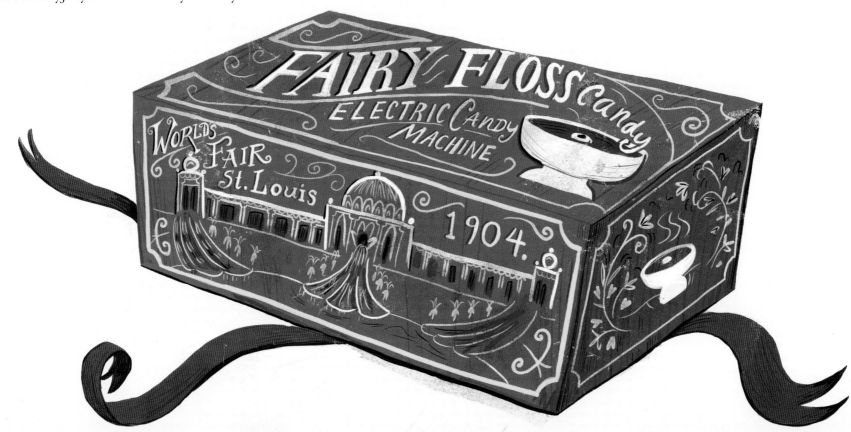